DIGITAL ART DECODED

A beginner's guide to create expression

Sarah Joshua

Table of Contents

CHAPTER ONE

INTRODUCTION

Individuals have used a get-together of magnum opuses over the whole course of all that working out to give their innovativeness and examinations. These cementing standard materials from former times to the fundamental level evident level headway in the tenacious day. Nowadays, experts have a tremendous degree of strategies to investigate. Some could go the standard course using paintbrushes, while others favor electronic workmanship, which uses make progress and workstations.

Certain level workmanship, as the genuine word frames, is depicted by electronic, especially robotized improvement. Pictures can be drawn the most expected disturbing way and sometime later isolated into a PC. They can to some degree be made using hardware, for instance, drawing tablets and a free open-source programming program, similar to Blender, or a paid programming program like Adobe Makeshop. Clear level workmanship has made to make obliging activity's, found in obvious Pixar films. Other present day mechanized expressive verbalizations join 3D sculptural renderings, control of make pictures, as well as a blend of various new developments. On a particularly basic level, electronic workmanship is a method for mixing craftsmanship and improvement that is obviously reasonable for sight and sound presentations since it might be found in various ways, including TV, internet, and online redirection.

OUTLINE OF 3D CONVEYING

Mechanized Workmanship Styles

As progress continues to grow, so does robotized workmanship. Coming up next such electronic workmanship styles.

Fractal/Algorithmic Workmanship

Fractal workmanship uses laptops to regulate non-straight and polynomial states of fractal structures, and the results produce pictures and visuals.

Data Moshing

This correspondence controls media reports to convey the ideal visual outcomes or pictures when the record is being decoded. It makes a mix of lodgings and irrefutable sadness of pictures.

Dynamic Inventive creation

It is one of the most present day and major level kinds of robotized craftsmanship. The craftsmanship is painted by a PC, in this way requiring unessential ensured work by the virtuoso a.k.a. the expert.

2D PC Depictions

It changes 2D layered models like messages and immense level pictures into 2D PC depictions. It's used in news sources and all that considered on standard outlines like typography, map making, express drawing, and publicizing.

3D PC Plans

It's a changed sort of 2D PC plans as it renders 2D graphs by really focusing on the three-layered piece of numerical data found in models or plans.

Pixel craftsmanship

This technique for best in class workmanship uses programming to make craftsmanship at the pixel level. The pixels are at times related for a retro appearance. Such a frameworks is gotten from 8-cycle and 16-digit workstations and PC game control place.

Essential level Make graphy

Different levels of progress produce electronic or PC based make graph to get, make, change and idea essential level pictures and make graphs. This remarkable workmanship style makes, appropriates, or uses robotized make graphs on laptops and the internet.

DIGITAL ORCA

Digital Art: History

Yet the verbalization 'progressed workmanship' was first used during the 1980s in relationship with an early PC painting program, its story follows as far as possible back to the 1950s.

Here is a course of occasions of its turn of events.

1950s

Computers recently came around during the 1940s when the Electronic Numerical Integrator and PC, or the ENIAC, was made for military purposes. Various trained professionals and originators began working with mechanical contraptions and basic laptops during the 1950s. They were early pioneers that arranged to electronic trailblazers. In 1952, a specialist, made 'Oscillon 40' using an oscilloscope to control electronic undulating waves shaped by an electronic sign.

1960s

Barely any people moved toward computers during the 1960s as they were expensive. They were typical simply in universities, research labs, and immense organizations. So it's nothing surprising that scientists and mathematicians rushed to attempt imaginatively with them. Clearly, they made their undertakings and used a plotter or impact printer to yield their indications. The point of convergence of their underlying works was high difference numerical designs and plans. A PC pioneer, Some time back, he made perhaps of the most baffling algorithmic work, a screen print of a plotter drawing called 'Respect à Paul Klee 13/9/65 Nr.2', which was stirred by one of Klee's oil-materials called 'Highroads and Byroads' (1929).

Toll Exploration focuses

The emerging American PC craftsmanship scene was strongly maintained by Toll Labs, making various automated workmanship pioneers. Among the specialists and PC scientists used. Billy Klüver was a fashioner who outlined Preliminaries in Craftsmanship and Development

(EAT) collectively with Robert Rauschenberg. Various subject matter experts and specialists used the equipment at Toll Labs out of hours. The exploration habitats developed early PC made exuberance. Leon Harmon and Ken Knowlton's Assessments in Acumen, 1967, generally called Bare, transformed into the famous works conveyed by Ring Labs.

1970s

At this moment, various skilled workers started to prepare themselves to program rather than teaming up with programmers. One of just a small bunch of remarkable foundations that totally coordinated computers and craftsmanship into its showing instructive program during the 1970s was the Slade School of Workmanship, School of London. A division called 'Exploratory and Handling Office' was made with in-house PC resources first class by various foundations. Paul Brown, who gained at the Slade from 1977 to 1979, encouraged a tile-based picture making system. His PC made drawings considering a direct plan of rules allowed individual parts to create or incite. Macintosh and Microsoft came in the last piece of the 1970s, making the essential laptops sensible and moderate.

Drawing tablet

1980s

Laptops entered associations and homes, transforming into a piece of ordinary everyday presence. Popular movies, for instance, 'Star Excursion II: The Fury of Khan' and 'Tron' both conveyed in 1982, and television programs used PC plans and embellishments. Accounts, computer games, and figuring advancement exploded in conspicuousness. Inkjet printers created as the most affordable strategy for engraving in assortment. It turned out to be more direct to make progressed pictures with off-the-rack paint programming groups. Clearly a 'PC up-to-date' entered standard society.

The 1990s to say the least

Nowadays, it's become obsolete to use 'PC Workmanship' to insinuate progressed subject matter experts and designers. Various experts as of now work in an irrefutably interdisciplinary way using different traditional and present day devices proportionally. One such specialist is both a modernized expert and a painter. Since the last piece of the 1980s, the skilled worker has been uniting the PC with drawings, syntheses, and makegraphy. How he blends the various mediums can make it trying to perceive the genuine paint and modernized paint. His specialty is reliably exceptional in pen, pencil, or watercolor, and he uses programming packs, for instance, Craftsman and Makeshop to examine mechanized subjects or straight stamps and models. The peculiarity of the "high level" in workmanship has worn off as development has become more general. In the modernized age, it is regular to see sensible, make, internet, and online diversion craftsmanship made with cutting edge gadgets and media without a significant relationship with the high level workmanship improvement. Today, these sorts of works are ordinarily named "new media workmanship." All things considered, high level workmanship has been misjudged until the new methodology of NFTs, Non-Fungible Token, which grant modernized assets for be tradable in the mechanized world. Especially like money, a fungible asset has units that can be traded.

NFTs give a superior way to deal with experts to sell their mechanized indications directly to craftsmanship epicureans. It's a genuinely inventive rebellion.

CHAPTER TWO

DIRECT PIXEL SPECIALTY OF AN ARCADE GAME MACHINE

Model Abstract

Individuals have used a variety of masterpieces over the whole process of everything working out to convey their imaginativeness and contemplations using different gadgets and methods: normal material and current. The methodology of computers during the 1940s arranged for cutting edge craftsmanship, which is depicted by electronic, especially automated advancement. It consolidates workmanship and development.

1. Programming programs

2. Math

3. Electronic contraptions

Anyway, as advancement grows, new automated are styles are made:

1. Fractal/Algorithmic

Craftsmanship

2. Data Moshing

3. Dynamic Thing of beauty

4. 2D PC Representations

5. 3D PC Representations

6. Pixel craftsmanship

7. High level Makegraphy

From the 1950s right up to this point, high level craftsmanship has continued to create. Electronic contraptions have become ordinary things with state of the art gadgets to make and share craftsmanship.

AUTOMATED WORKMANSHIP CONTEMPLATIONS FOR NOVICES

Creative mind doesn't seem to have an end. Regardless, on occasion, when the mind is loaded with such countless contemplations and thoughts, it turns out to be difficult to make intriguing show-stopper. For this article, I've accumulated presumably amazing and least complex modernized workmanship considerations for beginners to test. Keep on examining.

Key Significant focuses

1. Give your mind space for novel intends to come. Expecting your mind is involved, it's hard to determine what to draw.

2. Have a go at combining a couple attracting considerations the occasion that one isn't cutting it.

3. Have a momentous idea every time to keep your cerebrum open to new entryways and ways to deal with doing modernized craftsmanship.

Redraw Challenge

Outcome of a redraw challenge, Regularly we keep on looking for additional cutting-edge thoughts or considerations that transform into impasse. I would propose getting an ongoing drawing you made as of now and changing it. Whether it's a logo, an individual, or an image, you will be stunned to see the results. For trained professionals, there is no restriction to the inventive brain; this communication will positively make you experience it. I've been doing these 'draw this again' challenges beforehand and want to annihilate them the future too. They are clowning around, and you can agreeably see how you've progressed over the long haul.

INSPIRATION FROM ANIMALS

Endeavor to attract a fish as indicated by another perspective. You understand there is a particularly enormous sum in nature to stir us. While drawing characters, I could sometimes get inspiration from nature. Moreover, what interests me the most is the animals? You can start by drawing an animal and a short time later makes changes to its features or shades of it. In any case, do wide assessment on animals with relative figures and start drawing a remarkable creature or an animal starting there. Solidifying animal and human components will obviously make a truly new thing for the world.

Presumably the most favored animals on earth:

i. Canine

ii. Cat

iii. Fish

iv. Horse

v. Parrot

vi. Panda

High level Montage

A mechanized montage is a kind of visual artistic work made by joining different high level pictures and plans in a lone synthesis. It is an exceptional strategy for joining different memories in a solitary packaging. Modernized game plans can be produced using various sources, as makegraphs, outlines, surfaces, and models. They can in like manner consolidate text and other mechanized parts to further develop the general arrangement further. Numerous gadgets, similar to Adobe Makeshop, Craftsman, etc., permit you really to play out this when you work in the mechanized space.

Freehand Drawing

Quick sketch of an individual from Managing instrument Man. Particularly like you used to draw during your childhood days, you can use the electronic surface to restore your innovative psyche. Use the different contraptions and effects in your drawing in programming to redesign the drawings. I suggest you practice freehand drawing at a stretch and see the results yourself. Think about drawing and not such a lot regarding the last picture. To be sure, even layouts can transform into the last depiction. This is connected to liberating of making something last, this is connected to living it up from the chief brush stroke.

Portrayal

You can snap a makegraph of your friend, relative, or even a major name and sketch their image. It is reliably tomfoolery and easy to draw a portrayal. One of the most un-requesting approaches to drawing in a portrayal is to draw the singular looking forward to the watcher. Expecting that you are into it, mix different parts, like animals, nature, or such, to the image to make it truly intriguing and less hyper realistic.

Scene Drawing

This is something that probably all of you (experts out there) have done in puberty. Draw a mountain, ocean, or sky and decorate it with animals or dynamic parts. You can endeavor to empower the establishments by drawing in different parts to different layers, similar to the front, establishment, and focus ground to their own layers. Scenes for the most part give an incredible and intriguing feel.

Fan Workmanship

One of the most fantastic modernized workmanship drawing in considerations is to draw your brilliant calf or inspiration. It might be an entertainer, writer, lawmaker, business visionary, or liveliness character with whom you have respect or point of interaction. There is no doubt in the manner that you love them, so go ahead and make them with your specialist's hand. Yet again expecting you really want, you can moreover change their ruffle and various components, which gives the world a novel, new thing to experience.

2D Structure

Modernized show-stoppers are used commonly by reasonable craftsmen. It is a fundamental painting with no extra effects. It replaces hand drawings, as you can change and slapped together more while making 2D arrangements.

CTRL (CMD)+Z is one of my main backup courses of action concerning progressed painting, and keeping in mind that making mechanized craftsmanship, one of the most awe-inspiring things is how much experimentation you can do to achieve your work of art.

3D Material

The potential gain of mechanized workmanship is that you can do an amazing job and make 3D fine arts (in expanded reproduction or with 3D programming, like Maya or Blender). It resembles 2D materials anyway adds another layer of effects and significance to the drawing. It looks more reasonable and rich than 2D. You can put forth 3D fine arts for advancing attempts as connecting perfect with the crowd is known.

Doodle

Doodle tends to an unfocused drawing plan where hypothetical articles and shapes are used to make a compelling artwork. Essentially start drawing erratically and advance toward make a significant depiction. It is interfacing with and entertaining to do. Do whatever it takes not to mix this in that frame of mind, as in depicting, you can have a goal or the like, but with this, you don't. You essentially draw and let your mind take you to new spots.

Crossbreed Compelling artwork

This is where you join different expressive arts. For example, you can mix a trademark scene in with an image. Combination masterpiece doesn't have constraints and is a notable strategy for passing on a social or moral message. Causing to see environmental causes is for the most part used.

Mathematical Artistic work

You can use numbers and logarithmic or algorithmic pictures to make bewildering progressed workmanship. It can end up being valuable while managing guidance projects.

Numerical Shapes

The use of mathematical shapes in spreading the word about cutting edge craftsmanship is as numerical workmanship (one of various mechanized craftsmanship styles and types). A couple of numerical shapes can be utilized to make an enchanting piece of craftsmanship. Use direct shapes like circles, square shapes, and squares or complex polygons to make eminent models. Various craftsmanship programming has hidden shapes that you can add to your material and change further.

Adjusted Craftsmanship

Mandala craftsmanship, made with Fasten Studio Paint in around 5 minutes or something to that effect. Making even workmanship is horseplay and takes for all intents and purposes zero time. Various craftsmanship programming, like Catch Studio Paint, has an even ruler that you can use to make adjusted workmanship. Indeed, even workmanship is by and large conspicuous while drawing wonderful mandalas and mandala craftsmanship. In mandala craftsmanship, you make different shapes and models that all make this extraordinary (generally circle in shape) show-stopper with heaps of nuances. While using mechanized craftsmanship, you ought to just meddle with the even ruler settings and start characterizing limit workmanship. Straightforward and unquestionably fun.

Action Painting

This is a special kind of painting where assortment is erratically sprinkled and spread on the screen to give striking models.

Anyway it looks extraordinary; the use of automated advancement can give it a charming and present day feel. The key to making astounding action organizations is to use dynamic tones.

Make bashing

Make bashing is a captivating sort of electronic craftsmanship, but it is getting acclaim as it engages you to make sensible looking portrayals by hammering together extraordinary makes or 3D parts and protests to make your last show-stopper.

In make bashing, you can use craftsmanship programming, like Adobe Makeshop, to draw and paint on top of the hammered makegraphs to expand your imaginativeness and inventive brain moreover.

Themed Craftsmanship

Drawing with a subject by and large gives exceptional results. You can pick a point and base your characters, creatures, scenes, etc., besides, parts around it. For example, expecting your subject is fortitude, you can make electronic artistic work that unmistakably passes on this message. This ought to be conceivable by showing hands supporting each other or trees bowing in one course. Be permitted to pick and attempt various things with different subjects.

Subjects for your automated masterpiece:

1. Cyberpunk

2. Chess

3. Part like water

4. Wood

5. 8-cycle/pixel craftsmanship

6. Old style

Limited scope Thoughts

You can give a brilliant curve to your electronic masterpiece by making more modest than typical things. A fast model would be downsized individuals climbing a burger. Thusly, you can make a couple of fascinating electronic craftsmanship thoughts that look new and changed. You can assemble it concerning a subject or make it using a hypothetical setting.

Standard Pictures

Each culture has its practices and significant depiction. You can use them to make persuading modernized masterpiece that passes on a great message. These can be used in both thing arranged and scene organized electronic articulations. To add significance, research the importance of these pictures to stand further into considerations.

Indisputably the most known pictures on earth:

- Cross

- Star of David

- Bow moon and star

- Yin and Yang

- Emblem

- Ankh

- Pentagram

- Heart

- Skull and crossbones

- Token of generosity

- Fleur-de-lis

- Bird of prey

- Lion

- Legendary monster

- Phoenix

CHAPTER THREE

ASTOUNDING

DRAWINGS

You can take reference to popular milestones to make incomprehensible high level masterpiece. Investigate various roads in regards to them and put milestones from different central areas in a single packaging. Various promoters have used these designs to make stimulating modernized campaigns. You should in like manner investigate various roads in regards to this.

Unquestionably the most prestigious tourist spots on earth:

- Uncommon Mass of China

- Taj Mahal

- Pyramids of Giza

- Colosseum

- Eiffel Apex

- Model of Opportunity

- Machu Picchu

- Stonehenge

- Angkor Watt

- Christ the Deliverer

- Petra

- Moai models on Easter Island

- Burj Khalifa

- Splendid Entryway Framework

- Sydney Show House

Stream Effect

An effect makes a stream down completely search in your mechanized workmanship. The things or characters in your electronic craftsmanship will have a layer of assortment moving beginning to end, giving an enthralling spotlight on your work. You can add this to any of your electronic craftsmanship's.

Channel Effect

To make your high level workmanship look substantial, you can add channel effects on them. You can apply grayscale or monochrome channels to give a clear and dull tone. You can apply Unique, Oil Painting, or Craftsmanship channels for a more splendid tone. Channels can work on your mechanized frameworks and works by adding a layer of brilliance and finish to the drawings. In any case, manhandling them will definitely kill the spirit and soul of crafted by craftsmanship that your cerebrum and ability made. So try not to mishandle channels.

ELECTRONIC DRAWING EXERCISES FOR JUVENILES

For tenderfoots, modernized drawing in can be hard to learn and have an unsafe assumption to learn and adjust. Luckily, there are a couple of exercises that can help you with chipping away at your capacities. In case you do several these electronic attracting rehearses reliably preceding starting your specialty meeting, you'll be well on your way from a beginning high level skilled worker to a virtuoso. The best mechanized drawing rehearses for youngsters consolidate a lot of preparing with different sorts of lines, covering, and assortments. Ruling the basics can altogether influence further creating modernized drawing skills and making amazing workmanship.

We ought to make a dive and get everything going.

1. Characterize Matching Limits

Controlling your lines can be genuinely hard to overwhelm, but it's really critical for youngsters wanting to take their high level drawing in capacities to a more elevated level. Luckily, high level drawing programs like Imitate can make astounding lines and magnificent circles. Nonetheless, the thing may be said about all of various conditions of in the center between? Besides, do you have adequate control to characterize an exceptional limit, and a short time later draw another that intently looks like it? I like to practice this by pulling up a picture and outlining its state. The clarification I like outlining an ongoing picture rather than making your own is that it drives you to be considerably more controlled with your lines. For hell's sake, I can fudge my own appearances. "Point of fact, I by and large suggested for the head to be squashed like that". For sure, you can't pull off that while you're following. At the point when you've outlined your image, disguise the image and structure it again, including your most paramount graph as a helper and keeping a space of about a piece of an inch between them. Might you anytime make an undefined line to the first your made? It's serious, stress don't also if it's difficult every step of the way. Extra time, you'll get better at it and find that your line control limits have limitlessly moved along.

2. Meddle with Brush Strain and Thickness, One of the trickier things to become acclimated with automated drawing is the manner in which your pointer answers strain to extend your brush thickness. One second you're painting a fair slight line and the accompanying, you've pushed unreasonably hard and you have an enlarging mass in your once perfect line. To kick off, essentially go wild with your lines and pressures. To supervise them, you truly need to sort out how they

work regardless, and that suggests that some experimentation is all together. Change your brush to different sizes and see how slight and thick of a line this awards you when you either draw delicately or push down hard. At the point when you sort out how line thickness capabilities in the mechanized drawing world, you'll have much less complex time using it for your likely advantage.

3. Do an Outwardly hindered Structure drawing, blind structure drawing. Truth be told, research says that drawing an article

randomly will help you with drawing it non-unpredictably later (source). No, the assessment didn't use the word non-capriciously. Drawing an article blind helps you with killing your presumptions about what you figure a thing should look like and draw it as it truly is. You should pick between restricted choices when you were unable to look at your tablet. This exercise could have all the earmarks of being genuinely silly and moronic; basically trust me. Extra time, you'll start to see the benefits and improvements. I've truly created an entire post about the upsides of shape drawing and how it can deal with your art. Something fundamental can make a significant difference.

4. Assortment in the Lines, Concealing in the lines with concealing page. Without a doubt, I accept you ought to envision like you're a youngster again and start concealing. Actually, I genuinely love concealing at all ages. It's loosening up, silliness, and to be sure, truly incredible for your electronic abilities to draw. To the degree that mechanized drawing rehearses go, this is one that you can live it up with. Pick concealing

pages that you like and manage them like their own works of art. For hell's sake, even get them printed and illustrated when you're done. The support for why concealing is so ideally suited for beginning high level drawers is because it helps you with refining your precision and control. Envision your grade instructor persistently reminding you to assortment inside the lines. Concealing will similarly help you with becoming familiar with, taking everything into account, colors. Picking colors isn't for the most part as exceptionally normal as it shows up all along and truly takes a lot of deliberateness. Luckily, the accompanying mechanized drawing movement will help you with this capacity too.

5. Pick 3 Tones and Simply Use Those Tones, using tones with 3 concealed circles matching assortments can be dubious. It takes practice and experimentation. This exercise will drive you to be genuinely intentional about your assortment choices and simply pick ones that capability commendably together or not. Make a pass at working with only 3 tones at the same time. See how different assortments

coordinate and, when something looks off, what you truly need to change to make it right. You can kick off 3 circles, trading their tones until you feel like you have something sturdy. Then, at that point, have a go at drawing a picture, confining you to simply those 3 tones. How might they participate when they will undoubtedly detach circles? How might they work concerning a certifiable drawing? This exercise can furnish you with a lot of care while picking your assortments, which can be a colossal help to your electronic drawing life.

THE END